THE HEYDAY
OF THE DELTICS

Gavin Morrison

Ian Allan
PUBLISHING

Front cover: Gateshead's No 55 014 *The Duke of Wellington's Regiment* negotiates Chaloners Whin Junction, south of York, with the 12.40 Edinburgh Waverley–King's Cross on 19 August 1976. This stretch of the East Coast main line has since been replaced by a new line avoiding Selby. *Gavin Morrison*

Back cover: No D9013 *The Black Watch* departs Bradford Exchange with the four-coach Bradford portion of the up 'White Rose' Pullman to King's Cross on 11 July 1966. *Gavin Morrison*

Title page: Gateshead's No D9005 *The Prince of Wales's Own Regiment of Yorkshire* rounds the curve at Wortley Junction, south of Leeds, at the head of the up 'White Rose' Pullman on 30 June 1965. Just visible on the left (under the bridge) is the old steam shed at Copley Hill, closed the previous year; the tracks in the foreground (left) are the direct lines to Bradford via the Copley Hill triangle. *Gavin Morrison*

First published 2003

ISBN 0 7110 2960 1

Published by Ian Allan Publishing

an imprint of Ian Allan Publishing Ltd, Hersham, Surrey KT12 4RG.
Printed by Ian Allan Printing Ltd, Hersham, Surrey KT12 4RG.

Code: 0307/B2

Introduction

It is said that the basic design concept for what became known as the 'Deltic' (later BR Class 55) came from Lord Nelson, Chairman of the English Electric group, who had the idea of building a locomotive powered by two high-speed 1,650hp Napier Deltic engines as used in motor torpedo boats for the Royal Navy. As a result, English Electric commenced design work on such a locomotive in September 1951 as a private venture, construction starting in November 1951 at the Dick Kerr works in Preston. In October 1955 this prototype, appropriately named *Deltic*, started trials on BR, initially on the London Midland Region and later (from 1959) on the Eastern Region. Weighing just 99 tons but delivering 3,300hp, it was then the most powerful diesel locomotive in the world.

Main-line diesels for inter-city workings arrived on the East Coast main line in 1958 in the form of the English Electric Type 4s (later Class 40), and it came as no surprise that these heavy machines (133 tons) represented virtually no improvement in terms of performance over the large fleet of Pacific steam engines. ER management, ably led by Gerry Fiennes, was aware that, unless average speeds for inter-city trains on the East Coast services were raised to around 75mph, there would be an adverse effect on receipts, particularly as the West Coast electrification as far as Manchester and Liverpool was virtually complete, making times to Scotland very competitive, even when changing over to diesel traction

Left: Finsbury Park's No 55 003 *Meld* and Haymarket's No 55 013 *The Black Watch* await the coming week's work as they stand side by side at Finsbury Park on Sunday 31 July 1977. *Gavin Morrison*

Above: A very fine picture taken on 23 June 1959 of the impressive *Deltic* prototype powering away from Retford at the head of the 12.20 Hull–King's Cross, which it would have taken over at Doncaster. *David Marriott*

from Crewe. Consequently the ER, along with the North Eastern and Scottish Regions, persuaded the British Transport Commission to sanction an order for 22 production 'Deltics', at a cost of £155,000 per locomotive.

Due to a certain degree of wrangling between BR and English Electric over design details and equipment specifications, the class was a year late being delivered (which by today's standards seems quite good!), finally arriving from the Vulcan Foundry between March 1961 and May 1962; thereafter 'Deltics' would form the backbone of the ECML fleet until the

introduction of High Speed Trains in 1977.

Performance of the 'Deltics' was very impressive, and generally their capabilities exceeded the restrictions of the permanent way. However, like the racehorses after which the Finsbury Park locomotives were named, they required a high level of maintenance and a lot of money spent on them. Around 6,000 running hours for each engine was the target, which initially was achieved and even bettered, albeit at relatively high cost, but there were periods when availability figures were far from satisfactory, leading to the frequent appearance of Class 47s on 'Deltic'

diagrams. In due course there were 13 spare engines available, to keep time in Doncaster Works to a minimum.

The 'Deltics' were hardly ever transferred between depots until most of the class migrated to York for their last few years. Finsbury Park and Haymarket generally kept their engines in good external condition, whereas the Gateshead locomotives were often dirty, although I have heard it suggested that this was because they did more work!

Prior to 1977 the class were seldom seen off their regular routes and were extremely difficult to obtain for railtours, although the

No 55 015 *Tulyar* was selected to represent the class at the 150th-anniversary celebrations of the Liverpool & Manchester Railway. Diagrammed to haul the National Railway Museum's exhibits to the Bold Colliery site at Rainhill, it is seen passing Bradley Junction, just east of Huddersfield, with a wide variety of rolling stock on 21 May 1980. *Inset:* A close-up of the plaque commemorating *Tulyar*'s participation in the L&MR150 cavalcade at Rainhill in May 1980. *(both) Gavin Morrison*

occasional special outing did occur. After HSTs entered service they appeared on a regular basis at Hull, Cleethorpes, Aberdeen and on trans-Pennine workings, and were freely available for railtours; hardly a weekend went by in the last year (1981) when one of the locomotives specially prepared by York shed was not somewhere on a special.

The end (or so it was thought at the time) came on 2 January 1982, after which it was expected that those locomotives lucky enough to escape the cutter's torch would be seen in action only on preserved lines. However, the privatisation of the national rail network opened up new opportunities for the surviving 'Deltics', some of which subsequently returned to the main line. Their future on such work currently looks quite good, partly because of their 100mph capability, which helps them in obtaining paths on the main line, where such speeds are regularly attained by today's trains.

In 2003, in addition to the prototype, there are six survivors from the production series, four of which can be seen frequently on the main line, as well as making regular appearances at open days and at the preserved railways' various diesel galas. The time, effort and cost involved in maintaining these 100mph 'racehorses' should never be underestimated, so, if you have enjoyed a trip behind one on a special main-line outing, or been thrilled by the roar of Napier Deltic engines working hard on a passing train, why not join the Deltic Preservation Society by contacting the Membership Secretary at 36 Melbourne Road, Wakefield, West Yorkshire, WF1 2RN.

Many books and articles have been written on the technical details of the class, and Brian Webb's *The Deltic Locomotives of British Rail*, published in 1982 by David & Charles, contains probably all one would want to know. Having myself been involved with several black & white 'Deltic' albums over the years, I am delighted that Ian Allan Publishing has given me the opportunity to produce this all-colour album, although it is a pity that the class didn't last longer so that we could have seen what they would have looked like in some of the fine liveries that have appeared in the last 20 years; plain Rail blue was about as unimaginative a livery as one could imagine for such fine express locomotives. For those of you who knew the locomotives in everyday service, I hope the album brings back happy memories; for those who didn't, hopefully the pictures will give an idea of what 20 years of 'Deltics' was all about.

Gavin Morrison
Mirfield
March 2003

Above: The speedometer showing 100mph on No 55 018 *Ballymoss* between Peterborough and Grantham. *Gavin Morrison*

Right: No 55 003 *Meld* displaying the famous 'Flying Scotsman' thistle headboard at Finsbury Park on 30 July 1977. This headboard was not used during the blue 'Deltic' era. *Gavin Morrison*

Above: No D9000 *Royal Scots Grey* passes the site of Beeston station, Leeds (closed 1 March 1953), with a Leeds Central–King's Cross express on 29 June 1965. This was the first of the production 'Deltics' but the second to enter service, at Haymarket on 28 February 1961; named at Edinburgh on 18 June that year, it was nearly always selected by the depot for special events. Renumbered 55 022 in 1974, it would be transferred to York in May 1979 and would power BR's last 'Deltic' working from Edinburgh to King's Cross, on 2 January 1982, before being withdrawn and passing (in March 1983) to the Deltic 9000 Fund for preservation. It is now active on the main line. *Gavin Morrison*

Right: No D9001 was the first of the class to be delivered and arrived at Doncaster Works on 16 January 1961 for acceptance trials, during which it achieved speeds of 100mph down Stoke Bank. Eventually, on 6 March, it was sent to Finsbury Park depot, where it would remain allocated for its entire career except for about seven months spent at Haymarket from November 1967. It was not named until 7 July 1961, when it received the name *St Paddy* (after the racehorse) at Doncaster Works. In typical immaculate Finsbury Park external condition, it is powering away from Bentley near Doncaster on 2 June 1977 on the down 'Leeds Executive', which left King's Cross at 15.55. It would be one of the first two of the class to be withdrawn (the other being No 55 020 *Nimbus*), on 6 January 1980. *(both) Gavin Morrison*

ST. PADDY

Above: No D9002 became the first of six members of the class to be allocated to Gateshead, arriving on 22 March 1961. It was sent to South Gosforth depot for crew-training duties before starting its career on parcels trains to Carlisle. Having run without name for just over two years, it was named *The King's Own Yorkshire Light Infantry* in a ceremony at York on 4 April 1963; the name was previously carried by Class V2 No 60872, which was not withdrawn until 22 September 1963 and so ran nameless at the end of its career. The 'Deltic' was selected by the National Railway Museum as the example of the class for the National Collection and was presented to the public painted in the original green livery but with full yellow ends and numbered 55 002 on 12 December 1980, after which it worked the 14.15 York–King's Cross train. It had moved to York in May 1979 and would remain in traffic until 2 January 1982, being used extensively on railtours as well as

trans-Pennine duties. In spite of the number of heads at the windows, this is not a railtour but the 13.05 Liverpool Lime Street–York, seen passing Bold on 28 October 1981. *Gavin Morrison*

Right: No D9003 entered service on 9 March 1961 from Finsbury Park, where it remained allocated throughout its career except for a seven-month break from November 1967 when it was allocated to Haymarket. Like No D9001 *St Paddy* it was named at Doncaster on 7 July 1961 after a racehorse, in this case *Meld*. Having worked a down express from King's Cross, it is seen under the roof at Leeds Central before returning south on 3 March 1967. As No 55 003, *Meld* would be the third member of the class to be withdrawn, on 31 December 1980.
Gavin Morrison

QUEEN'S OWN HIGHLANDER

Left: No D9004 was allocated to Haymarket when it entered service on 18 May 1961 and received its name — *Queen's Own Highlander* — in a ceremony at Inverness on 23 May 1964. In the happy days of Pullman trains working out of Bradford Exchange, it is seen departing with the up 'White Rose' on 31 May 1966. Just visible above the nameplate is the regimental crest, as attached to nine members of the class, although many had vanished long before withdrawal. Latterly as No 55 004, the locomotive would remain at Haymarket until transferred to York on 13 May 1979 to eke out its days on far-from-taxing trans-Pennine duties prior to withdrawal on 1 November 1981. *(both) Gavin Morrison*

Above: No D9005 was the second 'Deltic' to be allocated to Gateshead, entering service on 25 May 1961, but was not named until 8 October 1963, when it became *The Prince of Wales's Own Regiment of Yorkshire* in a ceremony at York. Renumbered 55 005, it is seen passing Bridge Junction (just south of Doncaster station) at the head of the down 'Flying Scotsman' in wintry weather on 10 February 1978. As is apparent, the locomotive is rather dirty, which was not unusual for Gateshead's locomotives. It would be transferred in 1979 to York and repainted by that shed for working the '150th Anniversary of Mail by Rail' special from York to Liverpool on 11 November 1980, withdrawal nevertheless following on 8 February 1981. *Gavin Morrison*

11

No D9006 had been in service for only two weeks when photographed on 14 July 1961 passing Drem with what was probably a test or crew-training working. The locomotive was nameless at this stage and would remain thus for another three years, until 5 December 1964, when it was named at Cupar as *The Fife & Forfar*

Yeomanry. Latterly numbered 55 006, it would be based at Haymarket depot until transferred in May 1979 to York ahead of withdrawal on 8 February 1981. *Gavin Morrison*

No 55 007 *Pinza* passes Gilberdyke Junction at the head of the 08.05 King's Cross–Hull on 24 February 1981. It was named on 22 June 1961, the date it entered service (as D9007) from Finsbury Park, remaining allocated to that depot until its closure in May 1981; *Pinza* would thus spend its last six months at York, before being withdrawn that December. As can be seen, it has had its blue livery enhanced by the addition of a white cab roof — a feature of the Finsbury Park-allocated locomotives in later years. *Gavin Morrison*

No 55 008 had only 10 weeks to go by the time it was photographed emerging from the deep cutting at Marsh Lane Leeds with the 13.05 Liverpool Lime Street–York on 7 October 1981. As No D9008, this locomotive had entered service on 7 July 1961 from Gateshead, where it remained until moved to York in May 1979. At Darlington on 30 September 1963 it received the name *The Green Howards*, which had already been carried on 'Royal Scot' No 46133 and (in the singular form) 'V2' No 60835. No 55 008 would last to the end of regular 'Deltic' workings, finally being withdrawn on 31 December 1981. *Gavin Morrison*

With the cathedral standing out on the skyline, No 55 009 *Alycidon* heads the 17.46 Cleethorpes–King's Cross away from Lincoln on 12 May 1979. As D9009, this locomotive was named at Doncaster on 21 July 1961 before being allocated to Finsbury Park, where, apart from seven months at Haymarket from November 1967, it would stay until transferred to York in May 1981. The last of the class to receive a classified repair at Doncaster, early in 1981, *Alycidon* would have the honour of hauling the 16.05 King's Cross–York on Sunday 31 May 1981 — the last 'Deltic' working by Finsbury Park before the shed lost its allocation; needless to say, the locomotive was specially prepared for the event, with a special 'Farewell Finsbury Park' headboard. 'No 9' duly passed into the hands of the Deltic Preservation Society and can currently be seen in action on main-line specials. *Gavin Morrison*

15

Above: Looking well cleaned, compared to its coaches, No 55 010 *The King's Own Scottish Borderer* approaches Doncaster opposite the depot with the 12.05 King's Cross–Hull on 26 March 1981. The locomotive went new to Haymarket as D9010 in July 1961 but was not named until 8 May 1965 at Dumfries. Its main claim to fame is that on 16 January 1973, in just under 12 years, it became the first British diesel-electric locomotive to cover two million miles. In May 1979 it was transferred to York, where it continued to work until withdrawn on 24 December 1981. *Gavin Morrison*

Right: No 55 011 *The Royal Northumberland Fusiliers* protrudes from under the impressive roof of Hull Paragon station, prior to departure with the 12.34 to King's Cross on 4 February 1981. New to Gateshead on 24 August 1961, this locomotive was originally numbered D9011; it received its name at Newcastle on 28 May 1963. Like all other Gateshead- (or Haymarket-) allocated members of the class it was transferred to York in May 1979 and employed thereafter on trans-Pennine duties until withdrawn, in this case on 8 November 1981. *(both) Gavin Morrison*

THE ROYAL
NORTHUMBERLAND FUSILIERS

18 No 55 012 *Crepello* between duties in the yard at King's Cross station on 31 July 1977. As D9012 it was allocated when new to Finsbury Park on 4 September 1961, receiving its name at Doncaster on the same day. It would be one of just four 'Deltics' not to end its days at York, being withdrawn on 18 May 1981, just before Finsbury Park depot closed, albeit sent to York subsequently, to produce spares for the rest of the class. *Gavin Morrison*

No 55 013 *The Black Watch* heads a King's Cross–Aberdeen express past Rossington in wintry conditions on 16 February 1978. It went new on 14 September 1961 to Haymarket, where it would stay until transferred to York in May 1979, and on 16 January 1963 was named at Dundee West station by the Colonel of The Black Watch. In 1980 it would be specially painted by the depot to take part in the Liverpool & Manchester 150 celebrations at Bold Colliery, but in the event Finsbury Park's No 55 015 *Tulyar* would be chosen to represent the class. No 55 013 would be withdrawn on 20 December 1981. *Gavin Morrison*

Above: In an external condition typical of Gateshead, No 55 014 *The Duke of Wellington's Regiment* contrasts with the newly cleaned wall outside Bradford Interchange station as it prepares to leave with a train for King's Cross on 26 March 1979. One of six 'Deltics' allocated new to Gateshead, as D9014 on 29 September 1961, the locomotive received its name at Darlington on 20 October 1963. It would be transferred to York in May 1979, ahead of withdrawal on 22 November 1981. *Gavin Morrison*

Right: With the nearby works (or 'the Plant', as it was known) dominating the skyline, No 55 015 *Tulyar* passes through the centre road at Doncaster station with

the up morning 'Newcastle Executive' on 22 June 1977. New to Finsbury Park as D9015 on 13 October 1961 — the date it was named at Doncaster — it would stay until transferred to York in May 1981. In the meantime it would represent its class in the celebrations held at Rainhill in 1980 to commemorate the 150th anniversary of the Liverpool & Manchester Railway. To this locomotive would fall the honour of hauling BR's last 'Deltic'-powered King's Cross–Edinburgh train, on Saturday 2 January 1982, withdrawal following immediately. Passing into preservation in February 1984, *Tulyar* is now cared for by the Deltic Preservation Society at the Midland Railway Centre. *Gavin Morrison*

55 017

Class 55	
Weight tonnes	100
Brake force tonnes	51
ETH index	66
RA	5
Max speed mph	100

York
YK

Left: No 55 016 *Gordon Highlander* powers away from York and around the curve at Clifton with the 11.55 King's Cross–Edinburgh on 26 May 1978. As D9016 it was new on 27 October 1961 to Haymarket and received its name at Aberdeen on 28 July 1964. Aside from a seven-month spell at Finsbury Park starting in November 1967, it would remain on Haymarket's allocation until transferred to York in May 1979. Withdrawn on 30 December 1981, *Gordon Highlander* would eventually (in early 1984) be bought by the Deltic 9000 Fund and is now back in full working order. *Gavin Morrison*

Above: No 55 017 stands in the shed yard at York on 1 June 1981. New to Gateshead on 9 November 1961 as D9017, it remained at that shed until transferred to York on 13 May 1981. In the meantime, at Durham on 29 October 1963, it received the name *The Durham Light Infantry*, previously carried by Gresley 'V2' No 60964. The 'Deltic' would remain in traffic to the end, finally being withdrawn on 31 December 1981. *Gavin Morrison*

Above inset : The crest which York depot applied to its 'Deltics' at the end of their careers. *Gavin Morrison*

ROYAL HIGHLAND FUSILIER

Left: No 55 018 *Ballymoss* is seen well away from its normal routes as it passes Normanton station at the head of the diverted 09.30 Hull–King's Cross on Sunday 8 July 1979; the train would continue to Sheffield and then via Worksop, before rejoining the East Coast main line at Retford. The locomotive was new as D9018 to Finsbury Park on 24 November 1961 — the day it received its name at Doncaster. When 'the Park' closed in May 1981 *Ballymoss* would move north to York, remaining there until withdrawn on 12 October 1981. *Gavin Morrison*

Above: No 55 019 *Royal Highland Fusilier* poses outside its home depot of Haymarket on 5 June 1978; note the crest above the nameplate, and that this locomotive was numbered at both ends — at the time the only member of the class so treated. As D9019 it was allocated new to Haymarket on 11 December 1961 but ran nameless for almost four years; this was rectified in a ceremony at Glasgow Central on 11 September 1965, when it became the last of its class to be named. The locomotive would remain at Haymarket except when it was transferred to Finsbury Park between 3 December 1967 and 16 June 1968, until transferred to York on 13 May 1979. Withdrawn on 31 December 1981, it would pass into the care of the Deltic Preservation Society and can currently be seen working specials on the main line. *(both) Gavin Morrison*

25

Left: No 55 020 *Nimbus* heads the 13.00 Edinburgh–King's Cross past Rossington on 7 July 1977. Originally numbered D9020, it was allocated new to Finsbury Park on 12 February 1962 and received its name at Doncaster on the same date. In its early years it appeared to be Finsbury Park's favourite 'Deltic', but, as things turned out, it would be one of the first two of the class to be withdrawn, after a long period out of use at Doncaster Works, on 6 January 1980. *Gavin Morrison*

Above: No D9021 was the last of the class to be delivered on 16 March 1962, but did not enter service until 2 May 1962, and is shown here in the works yard at Doncaster on 29 April 1962, unnamed and in original two-tone green livery. Named *Argyll & Sutherland Highlander* at Stirling on 29 November 1963, it would be based at Haymarket except between 29 November 1964 and 26 June 1965 when it was at Finsbury Park until transferred to York on 13 May 1979, withdrawal coming in December 1981. *(both) Gavin Morrison*

27

Left: Gateshead's No 55 011 *The Royal Northumberland Fusiliers* prepares to negotiate complicated trackwork as it leaves King's Cross with the down 'Flying Scotsman' on 10 July 1976. *Gavin Morrison*

Above: No 55 005 *The Prince of Wales's Own Regiment of Yorkshire* completely surrounded by Class 47s in the locomotive yard outside King's Cross station on 10 July 1976. *Gavin Morrison*

Above: No 55 003 *Meld* races through the centre road at Peterborough as it heads north with the 12.00 King's Cross–Aberdeen on 16 October 1976. *Meld* would be the first of Finsbury Park's 'Deltics' to have the white cab roof added to its Rail-blue livery. *Gavin Morrison*

Right: No D9018 *Ballymoss* was only eight months old when photographed on 7 July 1962 climbing towards Stoke Tunnel at Little Porton at the head of the down 'Flying Scotsman'. Note the headboard. *Gavin Morrison*

Left: No 55 003 *Meld* bursts out of Peascliffe Tunnel, just north of Grantham, into the sunshine as it heads south with the 09.40 Leeds–King's Cross express on 27 May 1978. *Gavin Morrison*

Right: In the days when the signal gantries were still in use at Black Carr Junction, just south of Doncaster, Finsbury Park's No 55 012 *Crepello* heads north with the 13.08 King's Cross–Bradford on 6 July 1977. It would appear that the down slow line was out of use by this date. *Gavin Morrison*

Above: For 1977, to honour HM The Queen's 25 years on the throne, BR management decided to reintroduce the 'Silver Jubilee' name on the 07.45 King's Cross–Edinburgh and 15.00 return. Twelve headboards were made — six for 'Deltics' and six for Class 47s, in case of failures. *Crepello* hauled the first down train, on 8 June, and *Royal Scots Grey* returned with the up working. Here No 55 015 *Tulyar* crosses the River Don with the up train on 7 July 1977. The line from Hull can be seen in the background on the right. *Gavin Morrison*

Right: No 55 021 *Argyll & Sutherland Highlander* rumbles across the swing bridge over the River Ouse at Selby as it prepares to call at the station at the head of the 15.50 York–King's Cross semi-fast on 14 April 1981. *Gavin Morrison*

Above: In the days before the Selby diversion, when the East Coast main line went through Selby, No 55 011 *The Royal Northumberland Fusiliers* swings round the sharp curve at Chaloners Whin Junction at the head of the 14.00 from King's Cross to Aberdeen on 26 May 1977. *Gavin Morrison*

Right: Another picture of Gateshead's No 55 011 *The Royal Northumberland Fusiliers*, in immaculate condition just after an overhaul at Doncaster, heading for the curve at Clifton on the approach to York with an up afternoon express on 26 May 1978. Note that the headcode panel has now been plated over. *Gavin Morrison*

38

Above left: On cold nights the drone of the 'Deltics' could be heard for several minutes as they raced up and down the main line north of York. Here an unidentified member of the class heads south at Beningborough against an impressive sunset on 15 September 1975. *Gavin Morrison*

Left: Passing the pond at Raskelf, well used by local fishermen, Finsbury Park's No 55 012 *Crepello* races north through the Vale of York with a down express on 28 September 1975. *Gavin Morrison*

Above: Bensham, Gateshead, was a good place to see impressive 'Deltic' exhausts, especially when the locomotives were starting cold from Newcastle, as this tended to be the point where drivers started up the second engine. Here locally-allocated No 55 011 *The Royal Northumberland Fusiliers* gives an impressive display at the head of the 08.30 Newcastle–King's Cross on 6 August 1977. *Gavin Morrison*

Above: Alnmouth is one of the few places where the East Coast main line actually runs by the coast. The sea can just be seen on the horizon in this picture of Finsbury Park's No D9020 *Nimbus* approaching the station with an express from King's Cross to Edinburgh on the afternoon of 21 May 1966. *Gavin Morrison*

Right: Finsbury Park's No 55 015 *Tulyar* heads a King's Cross–Edinburgh express, probably the down 'Flying Scotsman', past Scremerston, about three miles south of Berwick-upon-Tweed, on 16 June 1978. *Gavin Morrison*

Above: After a brief stop at Berwick-upon-Tweed No 55 022 *Royal Scots Grey* heads for home with the 14.00 King's Cross–Edinburgh on 28 June 1976. The five-mile climb at 1 in 190 along the coast to the summit of Burnmouth Bank would present little difficulty to the 3,300hp locomotive. *Gavin Morrison*

Right: The most scenic stretch of the East Coast main line is probably the five-mile section north from Berwick-upon-Tweed along the clifftops to Burnmouth. Haymarket's No 55 004 *Queen's Own Highlander* climbs the 1-in-190 gradient at the head of the 12.00 King's Cross–Edinburgh Waverley on 6 August 1977, with the cliffs and the North Sea as a backdrop. *Gavin Morrison*

Left: The down 'Aberdonian', headed by Gateshead's No 55 017 *The Durham Light Infantry*, passes through the southern outskirts of Edinburgh near Millerhill on the evening of 3 June 1978. The train still had about 135 miles to go to complete its journey, which was 523 miles in total, although the 'Deltic' would be replaced at Edinburgh Waverley by a Class 47. *Gavin Morrison*

Above: Gateshead's No 55 002 *The King's Own Yorkshire Light Infantry* was selected by the National Railway Museum at York as the locomotive to represent the class in the National Collection. A year before withdrawal it was repainted in two-tone green but with full yellow ends, re-entering service in this livery on 12 December 1980. It is seen at Haymarket depot on 20 April 1981 awaiting its next turn of duty, which turned out to be the 17.00 from Edinburgh to Aberdeen. *Gavin Morrison*

Above: Having been informed by the running foreman at Haymarket that No 55 002 *The King's Own Yorkshire Light Infantry* was diagrammed for the 17.00 Edinburgh–Aberdeen, the author headed across the Firth of Forth to obtain this picture of the locomotive coming off the famous bridge on 20 April 1981. *Gavin Morrison*

Right: By 1981 there was very little work during the day for 'Deltics' that finished up at Edinburgh after overnight workings so it was not unusual for Haymarket to use one on a return trip to Aberdeen. On 20 April, having worked the 08.55 Edinburgh Waverley–Aberdeen, York's No 55 017 *The Durham Light Infantry* returned to Edinburgh with the 12.40 from Aberdeen and is seen here tackling the steep climb from Inverkeithing before entering the short tunnel at North Queensferry. *Gavin Morrison*

In the West Riding

Above: Leeds City station, in the form shown here, was about nine years old when this photograph was taken on 4 May 1976, having received a major transformation in 1967. No 55 015 *Tulyar* prepares to depart with the 11.30 to King's Cross. A second rebuilding has recently been completed, changing this location out of all recognition. *Gavin Morrison*

Right: The 1967 rationalisation involved the closure on 1 May that year of Leeds Central, which in its latter years did not offer passengers the most hospitable of travelling environments. On 2 July 1966, flanked by a Class 47 and a Class 101 DMU, No 55 015 *Tulyar* departs for King's Cross with the up 'White Rose'. *Gavin Morrison*

Above: Back in the 1970s fine photographic locations abounded on all routes radiating from Leeds, but sadly most have now been ruined by electrification. No 55 012 *Crepello* climbs the 1-in-100 gradient to the summit in Ardsley Tunnel with ease at the head of the 17.30 Leeds–King's Cross on 25 June 1975. *Gavin Morrison*

Above right: Haymarket's No D9021 *Argyll & Sutherland Highlander* has just completed the steep climb from Leeds Central to Wortley South Junction at the head of an up King's Cross express on 28 April 1967. To the left, by the third coach of the train, was where the direct route to Bradford Exchange turned left; below, to the right, can be seen the old London & North Western marshalling yard. *Gavin Morrison*

Right: Another photograph of Wortley South Junction, taken on 16 July 1976 from a viewpoint about 300yd to the south, showing No 55 012 *Crepello* at the head of the 17.40 Bradford Interchange–King's Cross. *Gavin Morrison*

Above: The sunlight is about to disappear from the cutting as No 55 004 *Queen's Own Highlander* emerges from the south end of Ardsley Tunnel with the 17.30 Leeds City–King's Cross on 23 September 1975. *Gavin Morrison*

Right: In the 1960s and early '70s it was extremely difficult to obtain a 'Deltic' for a railtour, as the class was fully diagrammed on the East Coast main line. Following the introduction of HSTs, locomotives were available at weekends, and on 23 July 1978 the ER's Sheffield division organised a 13-coach special from Sheffield to Carlisle over the Settle & Carlisle, hauled by No 55 003 *Meld*. The return working passed Engine Shed Junction, Leeds, just after 20.00, as the sun was rapidly disappearing. *Gavin Morrison*

Left: On 27 July 1976 No 55 017 *The Durham Light Infantry* heads the 17.30 Leeds–King's Cross past Lofthouse Colliery, scene of a serious accident on 21 March 1973 which unfortunately killed seven miners and resulted in the closure of the pit. This was also the location of the erstwhile Lofthouse & Outwood station, which closed on 13 June 1960; a new station would be opened by West Yorkshire PTE on 12 July 1988. *Gavin Morrison*

Above: Haymarket's well-cleaned No 55 019 *Royal Highland Fusilier* passes beneath the M62 motorway at Ardsley as it drifts down the hill towards Wakefield Westgate at the head of the 11.55 Bradford Interchange–King's Cross express 4 November 1975. The ex-Great Northern Ardsley steam shed was just a few hundred yards to the south of this location. *Gavin Morrison*

Left: No D9001 *St. Paddy* was only seven months old when it was photographed passing the ex-Lancashire & Yorkshire steam shed at Wakefield on 7 September 1961. The train is the 2.05pm all stations from Leeds to Doncaster, which was used regularly for crew training on the 'Deltics'. All signs of the old shed have long since vanished, and the site is now covered in large trees. *Gavin Morrison*

Above: No D9005 *The Prince of Wales's Own Regiment of Yorkshire* passes the erstwhile Kirkstall station, just north of Leeds, at the head of the 'Hadrian Flyer' railtour on 17 June 1967. This train covered the 86.8 miles from Carlisle to Skipton in 72min 47sec, which is believed to be a record time. Whilst this doubtless delighted those on board, management is rumoured to have taken a rather different view! The train would proceed south from Leeds at a more sedate pace behind Gresley 'A3' No 4472 *Flying Scotsman. Gavin Morrison*

Left: The 'Deltics' were regular visitors to Harrogate in the 1970s. A train that often produced one was the Sunday 16.00 from Leeds, which then formed a King's Cross working. On 28 May 1978 No 55 012 *Crepello* produces a fine exhaust as it accelerates past Wortley Junction before tackling the steep climb to the summit in Arthington Tunnel. *Gavin Morrison*

Above: An hour or so later, *Crepello* emerges from Arthington Tunnel with the evening Harrogate–King's Cross. *Gavin Morrison*

Left: The 'Deltics' were regular visitors to Bradford even before the new Interchange opened on 7 March 1977. No 55 022 *Royal Scots Grey* bursts into life before leaving with the 17.30 for King's Cross on 23 March 1979. *Gavin Morrison*

Right: The climb from Bradford Interchange through St Dunstans to Laisterdyke is mainly at 1 in 50, which on slippery winter mornings could cause the 'Deltics' (and other locomotives) a lot of trouble; times of around 30 minutes for just over two miles were not unknown. On 18 May 1977, however, the weather was fine as No 55 020 *Nimbus* rounded the sharp curve at St Dunstans with the 11.55 to King's Cross. *Gavin Morrison*

Left: Another photograph of the 11.55 Bradford–King's Cross, taken on 7 July 1976. Deep in the cutting on the 1-in-50 climb to Laisterdyke, No 55 022 *Royal Scots Grey* is seen between St Dunstans and Hammerton Street DMU depot, site of the one-time Great Northern steam shed. *Gavin Morrison*

Above: The 1-in-50 climb out of Bradford is over for No 55 012 *Crepello* as it passes the site of the former Laisterdyke station, which closed to passengers on 2 July 1966. The train is once again the 11.55 Bradford–King's Cross, recorded on 30 June 1976. Laisterdyke was once a busy junction, where the Bradford avoiding line to Bowling Junction left the main line to Bradford Exchange, and at the east end the lines to Idle & Shipley, Dudley Hill, Adwalton Batley and Ardsley, plus the loop to Pudsey Greenside, all parted company with the main line via Stanningley. *Gavin Morrison*

Left: In the late 1970s, following the introduction of HSTs on the East Coast main line, 'Deltics' became regular motive power on trans-Pennine trains between York and Liverpool Lime Street. On 23 July 1979 the rosebay willow-herb is in full bloom at Morley station as No 55 017 *The Durham Light Infantry* passes with the 17.05 Liverpool–York. In the background is the entrance to the 3,369yd Morley Tunnel. *Gavin Morrison*

Above: In its last months No 55 009 *Alycidon* received the silver-paint treatment from York shed but did not get white cab roofs. Here it is passing Mirfield, crossing the River Calder with the 13.05 Liverpool–York in lovely winter sunshine on 12 November 1981. *Gavin Morrison*

Left: An immaculate No 55 002 *The King's Own Yorkshire Light Infantry* bursts out of Gledholt Tunnel, just to the west of Huddersfield station, at the head of the 08.49 York–Liverpool on 20 October 1981. *Gavin Morrison*

Above: Looking up the Colne Valley towards Milnsbridge from the top of Paddock Cutting, one can see the viaduct in the background as No 55 017 *The Durham Light Infantry* descends the 1-in-105 gradient from Marsden at the head of the 13.05 Liverpool–York on 18 October 1980. *Gavin Morrison*

Above: In the last few months of 'Deltic' operation there was nearly always a railtour with the class at the weekends. York depot usually diagrammed the chosen locomotive for the previous Thursday's 08.49 York–Liverpool and 13.05 return, to check that all was well. On 17 December 1981 there was a good covering of snow at Ordsell Lane, Salford, and over the Pennines, as this picture of No 55 022 *Royal Scots Grey* shows. This view was taken from flats which overlooked the line but were demolished around 20 years ago. *Gavin Morrison*

Right: In the weeks leading up to the end of the 'Deltics' in January 1982, No 55 015 *Tulyar* ran several specials, and York depot seemed to apply more and more silver paint, until it looked really rather garish. On 22 October 1981 the locomotive is seen racing through Rainhill station at the head of the 13.05 Liverpool Lime Street–York. Note the plaque on the nose, commemorating its participation in the Liverpool & Manchester 150 celebrations the previous year. *Gavin Morrison*

Left: The West Riding branch of the Railway Correspondence & Travel Society was fortunate in securing No 55 007 *Pinza* to haul its special over the Waverley route on the last day of operation on 5 January 1969. This is a photostop at the remote Riccarton Junction on the outward journey to Edinburgh Waverley. The special returned in the evening ahead of the last train, the Edinburgh–St Pancras sleeper, which encountered considerable disruption *en route* from local people.
Gavin Morrison

Above: Following the disastrous collapse of Penmanshiel Tunnel on the East Coast main line in 1979, a few King's Cross–Edinburgh trains were diverted over the West Coast route via Beattock, but normally passengers were taken by bus between Dunbar and Berwick-upon-Tweed. Having been advised that No 55 013 *The Black Watch* would be kept on the train through to Edinburgh (rather than replaced at Newcastle by a Class 47), the author left Yorkshire in the very early hours to present himself at Gretna at 6.30am and was rewarded with this picture. With some spirited driving northwards, another picture was obtained on Beattock Bank. *Gavin Morrison*

Above: By 2 August 1980 No 55 011 *The Royal Northumberland Fusiliers* had lost its nameplate on one side. The locomotive is seen preparing to leave Scarborough with the Summer Saturdays-only 12.00 relief to Glasgow Queen Street — a duty performed by the class on a number of occasions. *Gavin Morrison*

Right: Another silver-paint job by York depot, this time applied to No 55 022 *Royal Scots Grey*, seen approaching Tinsley Viaduct near Sheffield with a special from York to Swindon and Paddington on 28 November 1981. Note the fine wooden headboard depicting this locomotive in green livery. *Gavin Morrison*

Preservation

Above: Along with No 55 019 *Royal Highland Fusilier*, No 55 009 *Alycidon* was handed over to the Deltic Preservation Society at a ceremony at Doncaster Works on 20 August 1980. It was chosen because it was the last of the class to receive a classified repair at Doncaster and was in working order to the end. Both locomotives were taken (by Class 37 No 37 100) to the North Yorkshire Moors Railway, where they remained for many years. 'No 9' is seen in action near Darnholme on 23 April 1988. *Gavin Morrison*

Right: On a visit to the Great Central Railway on 26 March 1994, *Royal Highland Fusilier*, by now bereft of nameplates and restored to original condition as D9019, heads south under the A6 road south of Loughborough with a late-afternoon working. *Gavin Morrison*

Left: Following withdrawal by BR in January 1982 No 55 002 *The King's Own Yorkshire Light Infantry* passed into the hands of the National Railway Museum at York. Thus far it has not ventured onto the main line, but it has made a few appearances at preserved railways. On one of these rare outings it is seen double-heading with *Royal Highland Fusilier* at Burrs Cutting on the East Lancashire Railway on 6 June 1996. 'KOYLI' is currently receiving a major overhaul, which has been in progress for some years. *Gavin Morrison*

Above: It was not until February 1984 that No 55 015 *Tulyar* was bought by Mr Peter Sanson and found a home at the Midland Railway Centre at Butterley. The locomotive has since visited many preserved lines; here, at Oxenhope on 6 November 1988, it is taking part in the Keighley & Worth Valley Railway's first diesel gala, the success of which came as a surprise to the line's management council. *Tulyar* is currently (2003) nearing the end of an extensive overhaul. *Gavin Morrison*

Above: No 55 016 *Gordon Highlander* leaves a trail of exhaust as it 'shuts off' on Mytholmes Viaduct during the Keighley & Worth Valley's first diesel gala, on 5 November 1988. This locomotive was the second to be acquired by the Deltic 9000 Fund, originally as a source of spares for D9000 but, as is often the case, was returned to working order. It has had a somewhat chequered career in preservation and is currently (2003) owned by Porterbrook Leasing. *Gavin Morrison*

Right: In 1982 'Deltic' enthusiasts would never have believed that the class would once again be used on regular service trains on the national rail network, but in 1999 Virgin Trains hired No D9000 *Royal Scots Grey* to work Summer Saturday trains between Birmingham and Ramsgate. Here, on 3 July, it races through Slough at about 100mph on the return working. For a limited period in 2000 No D9019 would do scheduled charter work, on the VSOE 'Northern Belle' service. *Gavin Morrison*

Following a lengthy overhaul at Brush Traction, Loughborough, for Porterbrook Leasing, *Gordon Highlander* was released for main-line working in 2001 in this striking purple livery. Whilst this may not be every enthusiast's idea of how a 'Deltic' should look, it certainly makes a change from the monotonous BR corporate blue! *Gavin Morrison*